Earth's Changing Climate

Understanding Climate Change

World Book
a Scott Fetzer company
Chicago

For information about other World Book publications, visit our website at www.worldbook.com or call 1-800-WORLDBK (967-5325).

For information about sales to schools and libraries, call 1-800-975-3250 (United States) or 1-800-837-5365 (Canada).

World Book, Inc.
180 North LaSalle Street
Suite 900
Chicago, Illinois 60601
USA

Library of Congress Cataloging-in-Publication Data
Understanding climate change.
    pages cm. -- (Earth's changing climate)
    Includes index.
    Summary: "Explains the science behind climate change, includes glossary, additional resources, and index."-- Provided by publisher.
    ISBN 978-0-7166-2706-7
    1. Climatic changes--Juvenile literature. 2. Global warming--Juvenile literature. 3. Nature--Effect of human beings on--Juvenile literature. 4. Global environmental change--Juvenile literature. I. World Book, Inc.
    QC903.15.U53 2016
    551.6--dc23
                        2015028042

Earth's Changing Climate
ISBN: 978-0-7166-2705-0 (set, hc.)

Also available as:
ISBN: 978-0-7166-2716-6 (e-book, ePUB3)

Printed in China by Toppan Leefung Printing Ltd., Guangdong Province
2nd printing August 2016

Staff

Writer: Jeff De La Rosa

Executive Committee

President
Jim O'Rourke

Vice President and Editor in Chief
Paul A. Kobasa

Vice President, Finance
Donald D. Keller

Vice President, Marketing
Jean Lin

Director, Human Resources
Bev Ecker

Editorial

Director of Digital Product Content Development
Emily Kline

Manager, Science
Jeff De La Rosa

Editors, Science
Will Adams
Echo Gonzalez

Administrative Assistant
Annuals/Series Nonfiction
Ethel Matthews

Manager, Contracts & Compliance
(Rights & Permissions)
Loranne K. Shields

Manager, Indexing Services
David Pofelski

Digital

Director of Digital Product Development
Erika Meller

Digital Product Manager
Lyndsie Manusos

Digital Product Coordinator
Matthew Werner

Manufacturing/ Production

Manufacturing Manager
Sandra Johnson

Production/Technology Manager
Anne Fritzinger

Proofreader
Nathalie Strassheim

Graphics and Design

Senior Art Director
Tom Evans

Senior Designers
Matt Carrington
Isaiah Sheppard
Don Di Sante

Senior Cartographer
John M. Rejba

Acknowledgments

AP Photo: 35 (David J. Phillip), 39 (Brennan Linsley). Richard Chandler: 29. Dreamstime: 31 (Matty Symons). Getty Images: 5 (Jonathan Kingston). iStockphoto: 33 (David Parsons). Minden Pictures: 43 (Sumio Harada). NASA: 7, 15 (ISS Crew Earth Observations experiment/Image Science & Analysis Laboratory, Johnson Space Center), 23 (SST/ Royal Swedish Academy of Sciences). Science Source: 19 (Karim Agabi), 27 (Chris Butler). Shutterstock: 11 (Sergey Andreev), 13 (Kodda), 25 (Krasavik), 37 (MaxyM), 41 (ArtisticPhoto), 45 (Jesus Keller). University of Northern British Columbia: 33 (Dezene Huber). U.S. Department of Defense: 21 (Lance Cpl. Joshua Murray, U.S. Marine Corps). Victoria & Albert Museum: 17. WORLD BOOK illustration: 9 (Matt Carrington).

Table of contents

Introduction 4

I. The Greenhouse Effect

Carbon dioxide 6

The greenhouse effect 8

The effect and life on Earth 10

Where do greenhouse gases come from? .. 12

Could volcanoes be changing the climate? 14

II. Global Warming

The Industrial Revolution 16

Carbon dioxide levels throughout history 18

Recent changes in Earth's climate ... 20

Could the sun be changing the climate? 22

III. Climate Change in Earth's Past

Studying past climate 24

Past changes in global climate 26

Why are scientists worried about climate today? ... 28

IV. Life on a Warming Planet

Effects of climate change 30

Mountain pine beetle outbreaks 32

The 2005 Atlantic hurricane season ... 34

How can such a small increase in
global temperature be dangerous? ... 36

V. Controversy and Consensus

Scientific agreement 38

Political disagreement 40

VI. The Future

Changing global climate 42

What can we do? 44

Glossary and resources 46

Index 48

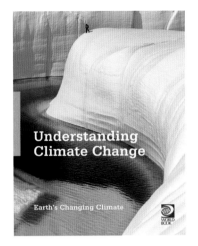

A scientist surveys the Birthday Canyon in the Greenland Ice Sheet.

© James Balog, Aurora Photos

Glossary There is a glossary of terms on page 46. Terms defined in the glossary are in type **that looks like this** on their first appearance on any spread (two facing pages).

Introduction

In 1958, scientists led by Charles Keeling at the Mauna Loa Observatory in Hawaii began tracking levels of a gas called **carbon dioxide** in Earth's **atmosphere.** (An *observatory* is a place where scientists study changes in the natural world.) These scientists noticed that carbon dioxide levels in the atmosphere were steadily increasing.

Reliable records for global temperatures reach back to the 1880's. These records show that the **average temperature** at Earth's surface has also increased over time.

In the 1980's and 1990's, a number of **droughts** (drowtz) and heat waves drew people's attention to a series of years of record warmth. The public became increasingly aware of an idea that had been developing among climate scientists— Earth's **climate** is changing.

The planet's climate is growing warmer. Much of that warming is being driven by the release of carbon dioxide into the atmosphere. And much of that carbon dioxide is being released by things that people do. The warming of our planet has already begun to affect our lives and will continue to do so. In a warming world, we can expect to see melting **glaciers** and rising sea levels. We can also expect increases in many kinds of very bad weather—not just heat waves but also **hurricanes** and snowstorms. In a warming world, it may also be more difficult to produce enough food and get enough fresh water for the growing population.

This volume covers the basic science behind climate change and discusses some of the possible effects of that change.

At Mauna Loa Observatory, scientists study Earth's atmosphere with a *laser* (a device that produces a powerful beam of light). The laser light is used to measure the amounts of certain *particles* (pieces of matter smaller than an **atom**) in the atmosphere.

Carbon dioxide

The story of Earth's changing **climate** begins with a gas called **carbon dioxide.** Carbon dioxide is colorless and *odorless* (has no smell).

Carbon dioxide is a very important gas. Green plants, *algae* (simple living things that inhabit oceans, lakes, rivers, ponds, and moist soil), and some other living things use carbon dioxide to make food. They take in the gas and combine it with water, using energy from sunlight—this is called **photosynthesis** (FOH tuh SIHN thuh sihs). Animals, on the other hand, produce carbon dioxide when they break down food to make energy. This is called **respiration** (REHS puh RAY shuhn). When you breathe, you take in oxygen and release carbon dioxide.

The chemical formula for carbon dioxide is CO_2. One **molecule** of carbon dioxide is made up of one **atom** of the element carbon, with the chemical symbol C, bound, or connected, to two atoms of the element **oxygen,** with the chemical symbol O.

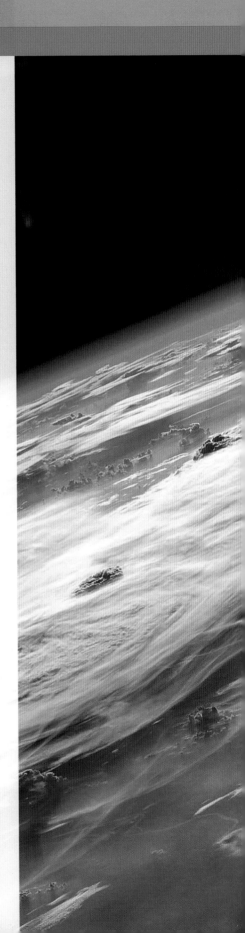

Carbon dioxide is made up of one carbon and two oxygen atoms.

A line of thunderstorms and clouds form in the **atmosphere** in a photograph taken from the International Space Station (ISS). Most of Earth's atmosphere is made up of **nitrogen** and **oxygen.** Carbon dioxide makes up only a small part of the atmosphere—less than one-tenth of one percent— but it has a large effect on climate. One way to think of that is, imagine that the atmosphere was equal to one dollar, then carbon dioxide would be one-tenth of one penny of that dollar.

The greenhouse effect

Earth's **climate** is powered mainly by the sun. The sun showers Earth with energy in the form of sunlight. The **atmosphere** *absorbs* (takes in) some of this energy. The rest strikes the planet's surface, warming the land and oceans.

The land and oceans, in turn, *emit* (give off) some of this heat back into space. But such gases as **carbon dioxide** can absorb this heat, holding it close to the planet's surface. This is why carbon dioxide has a big effect on climate, even though it makes up only a small part of the atmosphere.

This trapping of heat is called the **greenhouse effect,** because the gases involved act somewhat like the windows of a greenhouse. In a greenhouse, glass windows let the sunlight in. But they stop heat from escaping, creating a warm environment for growing plants.

Gases that contribute to this effect are called **greenhouse gases.** Carbon dioxide is a major greenhouse gas. So are water **vapor, methane,** and *ozone* (a chemical related to **oxygen** with the formula O_3). These gases help warm the planet's climate by preventing heat from escaping.

Rays from the sun

Most sunlight is
absorbed by Earth
and its atmosphere.

Some heat given off from Ear
released back into space, but
is trapped by greenhouse gas
warming the planet.

Some sunlight
is reflected by
Earth and its
atmosphere.

Other greenhouse gases

Human activities raise the levels of other greenhouse gases
besides carbon dioxide. For example, the greenhouse gases
methane and nitrous oxide are both present in nature. But
human activities have raised their levels in the atmosphere.
Scientists are most concerned about carbon dioxide, however.
They are concerned because about three-fourths of the
greenhouse gases given off by human activity is carbon dioxide.

The effect and life on Earth

By trapping the sun's heat, a greenhouse creates a warm environment in which plants can grow. Similarly, the **greenhouse effect** makes life on Earth possible for many living things.

Without the greenhouse effect, Earth would lose much more heat to space. The average surface temperature would be about 59 Fahrenheit degrees (33 Celsius degrees) colder than it is now. Many living things would struggle to survive in such conditions.

But too much heat can be a bad thing. Increases in **greenhouse gases** can cause the **climate** to change, placing living things under stress.

Many living things are highly **adapted** to a particular climate. Lizards and other cold-blooded animals, for example, rely heavily on climate to help maintain their body temperature. Living things also rely on a particular climate to provide the things that they need. Polar bears, for example, hunt and rest on sea ice. They rely on a climate that's cold enough to create and maintain that ice.

A lizard sunning itself for warmth. A cold-blooded animal cannot control its temperature using its body. It depends upon the temperature surrounding it to control its temperature.

Too close for comfort

Earth's closest neighbor, Venus, provides a dramatic example of the greenhouse effect. Venus is only about 30 percent closer to the sun than is Earth.

But Venus's average surface temperature is a scorching 870 °F (465 °C). Venus has a thick carbon dioxide **atmosphere** with clouds of *sulfuric acid* (a liquid that, when strong enough, is able to eat away solids and burn skin). These features trap great amounts of heat near the planet's surface.

Where do greenhouse gases come from?

Some **carbon dioxide** is naturally present in Earth's **atmosphere.** Much of this carbon dioxide erupts from volcanoes. In addition, tiny **bacteria** release carbon dioxide as they break down the remains of living things that have died. Animals and many other living things also breathe out the carbon dioxide they produce as they change food into energy.

Some of the carbon dioxide in the atmosphere, however, comes from human activities. People burn such fuels as coal, petroleum, and natural gas to make energy. These fuels are called **fossil fuels** because they are the remains of living things that died long ago. Fossil fuels are burned to power vehicles, to make electricity, and to heat buildings, among other things. The burning of fossil fuels releases a large amount of carbon dioxide into the atmosphere.

The clearing of forests for farmland or other uses also releases carbon dioxide into the atmosphere. This release happens more quickly if forests are cleared by burning.

Where carbon dioxide comes from

Carbon dioxide is often the by-product of combustion, or burning. A *by-product* is a secondary product created in industry. For example, people burn such fuels as coal and petroleum to produce a primary product, energy. These fuels consist largely of compounds, or mixtures, of the chemical elements carbon and hydrogen. As fuels burn, they combine with **oxygen** from the air, giving off energy as heat and light. Much of the carbon in the fuel binds with oxygen and is given off as a by-product, carbon dioxide.

Could volcanoes be changing the climate?

We know that the planet's climate is getting warmer. We also know that much of the warming is caused by rising levels of **carbon dioxide** in the **atmosphere.** Human activities release carbon dioxide. But so do volcanoes when they *erupt* (throw out lava and ash). Could volcanic eruptions be responsible for global warming?

Volcanic activity has certainly released carbon dioxide into the atmosphere over the last 250 years. But such releases have been much smaller overall than those caused by human activity. This makes a volcanic cause unlikely. In fact, large eruptions have a short-term cooling effect on climate. They release huge amounts of ash into the atmosphere. The ash blocks sunlight, cooling the planet's surface.

Mount Tambora

Mount Tambora, in what is now Indonesia, an island country in Southeast Asia, erupted in 1815. It was one of the largest eruptions in recorded history. Over the next year, places around the world had relatively cool and unusual weather. Some called 1816 the "year without a summer." Many crops failed. Some scientists think that the cold, wet conditions may have helped to spread several *epidemics* (outbreaks) of disease in the following months.

The caldera, or crater, at the top of Mount Tambora. The eruption of 1815 created this huge caldera, which is 3,600 feet (1,100 meters) deep and 3.7 miles (6 kilometers) across.

The Industrial Revolution

Human activities have always contributed some **carbon dioxide** to the **atmosphere,** even if just by people breathing or burning wood fires. But the rate at which carbon dioxide was released by humans grew rapidly during a time called the *Industrial Revolution*.

The Industrial Revolution began in what is now the United Kingdom during the late 1700's. Before that time, people made most of the things they needed by hand. They also used animals to power simple machines. During the Industrial Revolution, all of this changed, and people rapidly developed new machines and new methods for making things.

This change spread to other parts of Europe and to North America in the early 1800's. By the mid-1800's, industrial methods were widespread in western Europe and the northeastern United States. Industrial methods eventually spread to many other parts of the world.

The Industrial Revolution greatly increased the amount and variety of goods available to people. But industrial methods and machines require power. Much of this power comes from burning **fossil fuels.** People at the time did not realize that burning fossil fuels to power factories and machinery released great amounts of carbon dioxide into the atmosphere.

In a photo from 1857, the photographer Robert Howlett shows the construction of a giant steamship, one achievement of the Industrial Revolution.

Carbon dioxide levels throughout history

How much **carbon dioxide** has been added to the **atmosphere** by humans? Scientists measure carbon dioxide levels in parts per million (ppm). A level of 1 ppm means that there is one **molecule** of carbon dioxide for every 1 million molecules in the atmosphere.

Scientists can study ice cores (see page 24) taken from **glaciers** to learn about carbon dioxide levels. Ice-core data go back to about 800,000 years ago. Since that time, carbon dioxide levels have varied between about 200 and 280 parts per million.

Since the Industrial Revolution, carbon dioxide levels have gone up very fast. Carbon dioxide levels are around 400 ppm today. In fact, it took only around 100 years for carbon dioxide levels to climb from 300 ppm to 400 ppm.

A scientist studies an ice-core sample taken from a glacier in Antarctica.

How do we know?

Glaciers are huge sheets of ice found in the high mountains and all across Antarctica, the land that surrounds the South Pole, and Greenland, an island in the far north. Glaciers build up over time as snow falls, and the weight of new snow packs lower snow layers into ice. As each layer forms, it traps bubbles of air, preserving samples of the atmosphere from that time. Scientists drill into glaciers to get special ice samples called *cores*. They can study the gas trapped in cores to figure out how carbon dioxide levels have changed over the last 800,000 years.

Recent changes in Earth's climate

The rising levels of **carbon dioxide** have been matched by ever-warmer global temperatures. Reliable records of global temperatures reach back to the 1880's. Since that time, global **average temperatures** have been on the rise. From 1900 to 2000, global average temperatures rose by over 1 Fahrenheit degree (0.6 Celsius degree).

Recent years and decades have been among the warmest recorded. The 1980's became the warmest decade on record. That record was soon broken by temperatures in the 1990's. The 2000's were warmer still.

The year 2014 became the warmest year on record. At that time, 13 of the 14 warmest years had occurred since 2000.

How do we know?

In the late 1600's, some governments began setting up weather stations to track temperature, rainfall, snowfall, and other conditions. By about 1880, there were enough stations throughout the world for scientists to accurately measure global weather. Scientists can study these measurements to see how the climate has changed for over a century.

A wildfire in California in 2014. Unusually warm temperatures can lead to an increase in **droughts** and wildfires.

Could the sun be changing the climate?

We know that the sun heats Earth. We also know that the energy given off by the sun can be different at different times. Is it possible that current warming is caused by an increase in energy from the sun?

The energy given off by the sun *varies* (changes) in cycles that last decades. Cycles are things that happen in a regular way over and over again. However, these changes are rather small, and the cycles tend to be fairly regular. The sun is, in fact, a very stable, or unchanging, star.

Global temperatures, on the other hand, have not been varying in cycles. They have been rising more or less steadily for over a century, and maybe longer.

In addition, daytime and nighttime temperatures have not risen at the same rate. Nighttime temperatures have risen more quickly. If the sun was causing global warming, we might expect daytime temperatures to rise faster. The rise in nighttime temperatures suggests that **greenhouse gases** are keeping energy received during the day from escaping as heat at night.

There are several other lines of evidence concerning the sun and global warming. All of them suggest that the sun is "not guilty" of the current warming trend.

Global warming vs. climate change

The words *global warming* and *climate change* are often used to mean the same thing. These words are used to mean two very closely linked ideas. Global warming is the recent, *observed* (noticed) increase in **average global surface temperatures** on Earth. Climate change means the changes in **climate** linked to changes in average global temperature. Global average temperature has a complicated effect on climate. Global warming will not cause every place to get warmer. Instead, it will have a variety of effects on temperature, rain and snow, and other parts of climate. These effects are together called *climate change*.

This photo is of the central part of a *sunspot* (a relatively dark area on the surface of the sun). Sunspots appear dark because they are cooler than the rest of the sun's surface. Sunspots vary over a period of 11 years, which is known as the sunspot cycle.

Studying past climate

Global temperature records go back only a little over 100 years. To look further into the past, scientists must *analyze* (look at and think about) different kinds of evidence.

Some of this evidence is recorded in trees. Many trees undergo a yearly growth *cycle*—things that happen in a regular way time and time again. Cutting through the trunk of such a tree reveals a series of rings. Each ring represents one year's growth. Tree growth is affected by temperature, *moisture* (rain and snow), and other things. This fact allows scientists to "read" the rings, figuring out past **climate** conditions. Tree-ring data can go back hundreds of years.

Ice cores can also reveal past climate conditions. For example, the water in Earth's **atmosphere** includes different **isotopes** (forms) of the element **oxygen.** One form is lighter than the other. Water with the lighter form of oxygen generally falls as snow. Scientists can measure the amount of this isotope in ice cores to find out about past temperatures.

To understand climate as it was millions of years ago, scientists study fossils. Fossils are the preserved remains (bodies) of ancient things that were once alive. Different living things grow well in different living conditions. Scientists can determine what the temperatures were like at a certain time by the types of fossils left behind. Changes in the number of *marine* (ocean) fossils can also reveal changes in sea level, which are influenced by climate.

Changes in tree rings from year to year allow scientists to learn about such things as temperature and humidity at the time the ring was formed.

Past changes in global climate

Ice-core and fossil evidence show that global **climate** has varied greatly over time. The planet's history includes long periods that are fairly warm when compared with today. One such period happened during the time of the dinosaurs. This time, called the *Mesozoic Era,* lasted from about 250 million years ago to about 65 million years ago. Temperatures were generally warmer than they are today, and temperature changes from season to season were small.

Warm periods have been broken up by cooler periods called *ice ages.* During an ice age, huge sheets of ice spread to cover much of Earth's land. Periods of spreading ice are called *glacial advances.* Advances are separated by warmer *interglacial periods.*

The latest ice age is called the Pleistocene Epoch. It began about 2.6 million years ago. A great many scientists think we are still in this ice age. They think we are currently in an interglacial period that began more than 10,000 years ago.

An artist's illustration of what a frozen Earth may have looked like some 600 million years ago.

Snowball Earth

Between about 750 million and 600 million years ago, Earth underwent several extreme ice ages. Some scientists think the climate grew so cold that the planet's surface nearly or completely froze several times. This idea is sometimes called the "snowball Earth" theory.

Why are scientists worried about climate today?

We know the planet's **climate** has varied greatly over time. So why are scientists worried about today's climate change?

Over much of Earth's history, the climate has been fairly stable, or unchanging. And when the climate did change, it often did so quite slowly. Global **average temperatures** changed only a few degrees over hundreds of thousands or even millions of years. The current pace of warming is much quicker, perhaps quicker than at any time in the past 65 million years.

In the past, Earth's climate has had a few fairly quick changes. Like current climate change, these changes are often linked to rapid changes in **carbon dioxide** levels. Rapid climate change leaves little time for living things to **adapt** to new conditions. This can cause many kinds of living things to die off in large **extinction** events, forever changing life on Earth.

A photo of foraminifera (fuh RAM uh NIHF uhr uh) fossils, tiny ocean animals from the Paleocene (about 66 to 23 million years ago). During the Paleocene, 30 to 50 percent of foraminifera *species* (types) worldwide died out.

Climate change in the past

One rapid climate shift began about 56 million years ago, during a time called the Paleocene Epoch. At that time, carbon dioxide levels increased quickly. Global average temperatures warmed by about 11 Fahrenheit degrees (6 Celsius degrees). Much of the warming occurred over a period of less than 200,000 years. At the same time, huge extinction events wiped out as much as 50 percent of some branches of sea life.

Effects of climate change

Earth's **climate** is getting warmer, and scientists expect this warming to continue. Temperatures may rise by only a few degrees on average. Yet this small increase may cause large and damaging changes in the environment.

As temperatures rise, for example, many living things will struggle to survive in their current **range.** To maintain living in the temperature they like, some may shift their range closer to the north or south poles, to cooler temperatures. Some will not be able to shift fast enough. Others may find that their new ranges lack food, shelter, or other things that they need. Many species will die out, or become **extinct.**

Rising temperatures are already causing **glaciers** to melt. The extra water eventually reaches the oceans. There, it will cause sea levels to rise, threatening islands and coastal communities.

Rising temperatures will also put more energy, in the form of heat, into the oceans and **atmosphere.** There, it may lead to more extreme or surprising and unusual weather events. These are just a few of the possible results of climate change.

A marker in Jasper National Park in Canada shows how glacial ice in the Canadian Rockies has retreated in the last century.

The glacier was here in
Le glacier était ici en
1908

Mountain pine beetle outbreaks

In many areas, **climate** change may help pests to flourish. This may already be happening in the western United States and Canada. In the late 1990's and early 2000's, large numbers of pine trees in the West began turning brown and dying. The cause is a pest called the *mountain pine beetle.*

The female mountain pine beetle burrows into living pine trees, laying her eggs there. The *larvae* (young— LAHR vee) hatch and feed beneath the tree's bark. The larvae and a *fungus* (a type of living thing that absorbs food from the surroundings) carried by the larvae kill the tree. The beetles emerge from the dead tree as adults and spread to new trees.

Outbreaks of mountain pine beetles have happened from time to time in the past. But this latest one has grown to cover millions of acres. The loss of trees has harmed creatures that depend on them, damaging entire **ecosystems.**

Several things have contributed to the beetle outbreak. One of them likely is climate change. Extremely cold winter temperatures can harm the beetles as they shelter beneath the pine bark, reducing their numbers in following years. But this area has experienced a recent streak of relatively warm winters, probably because of global warming. With fewer beetles killed each winter, there are more to spread in the spring.

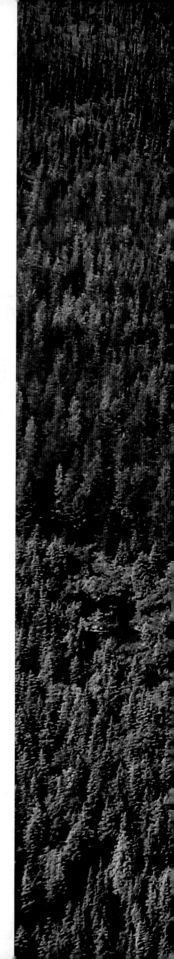

Over the past decade, the mountain pine beetle (see inset) has killed millions of pine trees in the western United States and Canada. Orange and purple trees shown in this photo from British Columbia in western Canada are dead or dying pines. Warmer winters have helped the insect to thrive.

The 2005 Atlantic hurricane season

Are deadly storms more likely in a warming world? Many scientists think that we can expect to see more powerful storms and more surprising and unusual weather events.

The **hurricane** season of 2005 could provide an example of times to come. During the summer of that year, more than two dozen tropical storms formed in the Atlantic Ocean. A record number of 15 of these storms grew to become hurricanes. Four of them reached the highest strength—called category 5—with sustained, or steady, wind speeds of more than 156 miles (250 kilometers) per hour.

One of these storms, Hurricane Katrina, crossed Florida and made landfall in New Orleans, Louisiana. There, a wave of water called a *storm surge* overwhelmed the city's flood wall system, flooding nearly the entire city. Katrina caused massive damage along the Gulf Coast. In all, Katrina killed about 1,800 people and became one of the costliest natural disasters in history. Another storm in 2005, Hurricane Wilma, became the strongest Atlantic hurricane on record. At Wilma's peak, winds inside the storm reached speeds of 185 miles (295 kilometers) per hour.

Hurricanes and climate change

Hurricanes and other tropical storms require warm ocean waters to develop. The release of **carbon dioxide** into Earth's **atmosphere** is leading to the warming of both the ocean and air temperatures. Some scientists think that extra heat helped fuel the historic 2005 Atlantic hurricane season. If so, we may continue to see more frequent and more powerful hurricanes.

Helicopters are used to rescue people from floods in New Orleans, on September 1, 2005, three days after Hurricane Katrina hit the city.

35

How can such a small increase in global temperature be dangerous?

Scientists predict that the planet will warm somewhere between 2 and 12 Fahrenheit degrees (1 and 7 Celsius degrees) by the year 2100. That may not seem like much. How can a change of only a few degrees affect our lives?

Remember that the increase will be in **average global temperature**—that is, the temperature of the entire planet. Even small changes can have a big effect when spread over such a large area. Also remember that Earth's **climate** is a complex system. So the climate of some areas will change much more than that of others.

Even if global average temperatures rose only 2 Fahrenheit degrees (1 Celsius degree), we could see crop yields grown using current farming methods drop by 5 to 15 percent. The heaviest rainfalls could increase by 3 to 10 percent. Two to four times as much land area might be burned by wildfires annually in the American West.

Also, remember that many living things are highly **adapted** to certain living conditions. A shift of only a few degrees is enough to force many living things out of their **ranges.**

It's called global warming, so why isn't it warmer?

People often talk about global warming as if temperatures every day and everywhere will rise. This is not necessarily true. Global average temperatures are rising, but not all places will grow steadily warmer. Some areas may see more extreme weather events and changing patterns of rainfall and snowfall. Certain areas will even grow cooler as the planet warms overall.

Scientific agreement

We know that **carbon dioxide** levels have been increasing in the **atmosphere.** We also know that global **average temperature** has increased over the same time. Could this be a coincidence? Of course. But we also know that carbon dioxide is a heat-trapping **greenhouse gas.** This fact suggests a meaningful connection between carbon dioxide and temperature. It helps scientists to design experiments and studies to see if rising carbon dioxide levels are contributing to the rise in global average temperature.

We also know that human activities, including the burning of **fossil fuels,** release tremendous amounts of carbon dioxide into the atmosphere. This fact allows scientists to study whether such *emissions* (gases given off) are contributing to **climate** change.

People once doubted that human activities were causing the planet to grow warmer. But over time, climate scientists have collected and weighed evidence. It has contributed to a growing *consensus* (general agreement) that climate change caused by human activities is real. Scientists differ on how much warming may occur over how much time. But despite this, the majority of scientists accept the reality of human-caused global warming.

A scientist releases a weather balloon from a research station operated by the U.S. National Science Foundation atop the Greenland ice sheet. Data sent from such weather balloons help scientists to understand the changes we see in our climate.

Political disagreement

Many people still deny that global warming is happening. But this disagreement is generally not scientific in nature. It does not come from a careful study of the available evidence. Rather, people have many other reasons to discount global warming. Many of them worry that people will try to fight climate change by reducing energy use. They fear that reducing energy use will hurt their nation's *economy* (the amount of goods and services made by a country). That could cause people to lose their jobs and become poorer. They also fear that government laws about the release of **carbon dioxide** into the **atmosphere** will harm businesses and reduce profits.

Despite these objections, scientists have a duty to weigh the evidence to determine what is really happening. Nearly all climate scientists agree that present warming is the result of human activities. Climate change disbelievers remain. But, they must provide science-based evidence in support of their position to change what most scientists, and many other people, now think about climate change.

A global organization for a global problem

In 1988, the United Nations created the Intergovernmental Panel on Climate Change (IPCC) to investigate climate-change research being published and determine its main points. Thousands of scientists voluntarily contribute to the IPCC's reports. In 2007, the IPCC reported that it was certain that Earth was warming and that it was 90 percent certain that human activities were the main cause. In its 2014 report, the IPCC upgraded the chance that human activities are changing the climate to "extremely likely," a certainty of 95 percent.

Changing global climate

What does the future hold for Earth's climate? Most scientists agree that we can expect global **average surface temperatures** to rise by at least about 0.3 Fahrenheit degree (0.2 Celsius degree) each decade for the future we can know about. The temperature could rise up to 7 Fahrenheit degrees (4 Celsius degrees) or more in the next 100 years.

Such a major change over a short time will likely lead to an increase in severe weather events. Warming temperatures will cause **habitats** to shift, putting wildlife under stress. Melting ice will raise sea levels, threatening low-lying coastal areas. Rising temperatures will also challenge our ability to provide the food and water that people need.

The amount and rate of warming will depend in part on the level of **greenhouse gases** we release into the **atmosphere.** Human activities have led to a continuing increase in the release of greenhouse gases since the Industrial Revolution. If this continues, global average temperatures will likely increase more quickly. If we can reduce the amounts of greenhouse gases released into the atmosphere, warming will likely occur more slowly. Temperature changes tend to follow behind changes in greenhouse gas levels. So even if we could somehow stop releasing greenhouse gases entirely, temperatures would continue to rise for a time.

Pikas (PY kuhz) are related to the rabbit. The American pika lives on cold mountaintops in the Western United States. The warming climate is causing pikas that live below an *elevation* (height) of 7,000 feet (2,133 meters) to die off.

What can we do?

The planet has already begun to warm and will continue to do so. We can limit future warming by reducing the amount of **carbon dioxide** we put into the **atmosphere.** There is a role for everyone to play in this effort. At home, we can help by saving energy. Engineers and scientists are working on more efficient ways to use energy. They are also developing different energy sources, such as wind power and solar power, that do not produce energy by the *combustion* (burning) of **fossil fuels.** Industries are also developing ways to capture carbon dioxide in underground storage, rather than releasing it into the atmosphere.

Scientists will also have to develop ways to deal with the effects of global warming. They will have to figure out how to produce food more effectively in changing growing conditions.

Scientists may even have to investigate extreme ideas to cool the planet. Some scientists are working on ideas that would increase cloud cover or place reflectors around the planet, sending more of the sun's energy into space. Such solutions would be difficult and costly, but if warming continues, we may have little choice.

Kyoto and Paris

One of the major challenges of **climate** change is that it is a global problem. It does little good for one nation to reduce the level of carbon dioxide it releases if others are increasing theirs. In the late 1990's, an agreement called the Kyoto (kee OH toh) Protocol (PROH tuh kol), named for the Japanese city of Kyoto, was put together. The protocol called on nations to limit their release of carbon dioxide into the atmosphere. It was difficult to get nations to agree to the protocol, and some, including the United States, never did. The protocol ended in 2012. In 2015, 195 countries adopted the Paris Agreement, which will replace the Kyoto Protocol. For the agreement to take effect, at least 55 members of the UN Framework Convention on Climate Change (UNFCCC) representing at least 55 percent of total global greenhouse gases must sign on. Environmentalists hope the Paris Agreement's combination of required emission reviews and voluntary acts will do more to reduce global warming.

adapt For a living thing to change in structure, form, or habits to fit different conditions.

atmosphere The mass of gases that surrounds a planet.

atom The building blocks of the simplest kinds of matter on Earth, the chemical elements. Elements include hydrogen and oxygen. Each element is made of one basic kind of atom.

average temperature A temperature for a given time period. For example, in a month, the temperature for each day is totaled, and that number is divided by the number of days in the month, to get the average temperature.

bacteria Simple living things made up of one cell.

carbon dioxide A colorless, *odorless* (with no smell) gas found in the atmospheres of many planets, including Earth. On Earth, green plants must get carbon dioxide from the atmosphere to live and grow. Animals produce the gas when their bodies convert food into energy, then release carbon dioxide into the atmosphere. Carbon dioxide is also created by burning things that contain the chemical element carbon.

climate The weather of a place averaged over a length of time.

drought When the average rainfall for an area drops far below normal for a long time.

ecosystem A system made up of a group of living beings and their environment.

extinct When every member of a *species* (kind) of living thing has died.

fossil fuel An energy-providing material—coal, oil, or natural gas—formed from the long-dead *remains* (bodies) of living things.

glacier A large mass of ice that moves slowly because of gravity.

greenhouse effect A warming of the lower atmosphere and surface of a planet by a process involving sunlight, gases, and atmospheric particles. On Earth, the greenhouse effect began long before humans existed. However, the amounts of heat-trapping atmospheric gases, called greenhouse gases, have increased since the mid-1800's, when modern industry became widespread.

habitat The kind of place that a living thing prefers.

hurricane A powerful, swirling storm that begins over a warm sea.

isotope One of two or more atoms of the same chemical element that differ in the amount of matter they contain. All of an element's isotopes have the same number of *protons* (positively charged particles) but a different number of *neutrons* (electrically neutral particles).

methane A colorless, odorless, flammable gas.

molecule The smallest amount into which something can be divided and still have the chemical make-up of the original substance.

nitrogen A chemical element (N) that occurs in nature as a colorless, odorless, and tasteless gas.

oxygen A chemical element (O) that is one of the most plentiful elements on Earth.

photosynthesis A food-making process. In photosynthesis, green plants and some other living things use sunlight to combine carbon dioxide and water to make food.

range The geographic area in which an animal or plant species may be found.

respiration The way that human beings and other living things get and use oxygen.

vapor The gas state that solids and liquids become when heated. When water is heated to create steam, the steam is a vapor.

Books:

Bang, Molly, and Penny Chisholm. *Buried Sunlight: How Fossil Fuels Have Changed the Earth.* New York: The Blue Sky Press, 2014.

Green, Dan, and Simon Basher. *Climate Change.* New York: Kingfisher, 2014.

Miller, Debra A. *Global Warming.* Detroit: Greenhaven, 2013.

Rothschild, David de. *Earth Matters.* New York: DK Pub., 2011.

Tomecek, Steve. *Global Warming and Climate Change.* New York: Chelsea House, 2012.

Websites:

NASA – Climate Change and Global Warming
http://climate.nasa.gov/

National Geographic – Global Warming
http://environment.nationalgeographic.com/environment/global-warming/

National Park Service – Climate Change
http://www.nps.gov/subjects/climatechange/

United States Environmental Protection Agency – A Student's Guide to Global Climate Change
http://www.epa.gov/climatestudents/

Think about it:

Since the sun heats Earth with its energy, some people have argued that the sun is causing global warming and not humans. Can you give two reasons why this is unlikely?

1) The energy from the sun increases and decreases in fairly steady cycles. But the warming we have seen on Earth has not risen and fallen. It has risen steadily for a century or more. 2) And, if the sun really were causing global warming, we would expect to see greater increases in temperature during the day, as the sun's effect is greater during daytime. However, scientists have measured that nighttime global temperatures have risen at a faster rate than daytime temperatures.

A

adaptation, 10, 28, 36
animals and plants. *See* living things
atmosphere, 4, 7, 8-9, 30, 42; of Venus, 11
average temperatures, 10, 28, 29, 42; global warming and, 4, 20-21, 23, 36-39

B

bacteria, 12
beetles, mountain pine, 32-33
burning. *See* combustion

C

carbon dioxide, 4, 11, 28, 35; as gas, 6, 7; in greenhouse effect, 8-9, 38; levels through history, 18-19; reducing levels, 44-45; sources of, 12-17
climate, 8; studying, 24-25
climate change, 4, 23; insect pests and, 32-33; past, 26-29. *See also* global warming
combustion, 12, 13, 21

D

droughts, 4, 21

E

extinction, 28-30

F

foraminifera, 29
fossil fuels, 12-13, 16, 38, 44
fossils, 24, 26

G

glacial advances, 26
glaciers, 4, 18-19, 30-31

global warming, 4; causes of, 12-17, 22-23; controversy over, 38-41; dealing with, 44-45; effects of, 10-11, 30-37; in future, 42-43; recent changes in, 20-21, 28, 29
greenhouse effect, 8-9, 22, 38, 42; living things and, 10-11; origin of gases, 12-13
Greenland, 19

H

habitats, 42
heat waves, 4
hurricanes, 4, 34-35; Katrina, 34-35; Wilma, 34

I

ice, 4, 30-31; core studies, 18-19, 24, 26
ice ages, 26, 27
Industrial Revolution, 16-18, 42
interglacial periods, 26
Intergovernmental Panel on Climate Change (IPCC), 41

K

Keeling, Charles, 4
Kyoto Protocol, 45

L

living things, 6, 24; global warming effects on, 10-11, 28-30, 32-33, 36, 42
lizards, 10-11

M

Mauna Loa Observatory, 4, 5
Mesozoic Era, 26
methane, 8, 9
Mount Tambora, 14-15

N

New Orleans, 34-35
nitrogen, 7

O

oxygen, 6-7; isotopes of, 24

P

Paleocene Epoch, 29
Paris Agreement, 45
pests, 32-33
photosynthesis, 6
pikas, 43
Pleistocene Epoch, 26

R

ranges, 30, 36
respiration, 6

S

scientists, 28, 38-41
snowball Earth theory, 27
sun, 8-9, 22-23, 44, 47
sunspots, 23

T

tree rings, 24-25

V

Venus, 11
volcanoes, 14-15

W

weather, 4, 7, 34-35, 37, 42
weather balloons, 39
wildfires, 20-21, 36